W9-BLO-543

A Gift For:

From:

momISMS

WHAT SHE SAYS AND WHAT SHE REALLY MEANS

by Cathy Hamilton

GIFT BOOKS
from Hallmark

Andrews McMeel Publishing, LLC

BOK4322

This edition published in 2006 by Andrews McMeel Publishing, LLC,
exclusively for Hallmark Cards, Inc.

www.Hallmark.com

ISBN: 0-7407-6518-3

Book design by Holly Camerlinck

To my mother, Mignon,
a loving woman with a wonderful
sense of humor who would like
readers to know she never once
told any of her five kids to
"Go out and play in traffic"

"Don't use that tone of voice with me, young lady (man)!"

This ism stems from every mom's firm belief that she is the only one in the household entitled to use an authoritative tone of voice. The privilege of "tone" is not afforded even to husbands, let alone children. It is "tone" that gives Mom her power. It is exclusively hers. To lose tone would be to lose everything.

"Just use your own judgment. I trust you."

{ Pronounced with all the conviction a mom can muster before she leaves the kids alone in the house for the evening or, God forbid, a weekend, this statement is a preemptive strike meant to impose guilt before anything bad actually happens. }

It rarely works.

"Is that what you're going to wear?"

{ Used indiscriminately for sons, daughters, and husbands, this one is a not-so-subtle attempt to make family members rethink their wardrobe choice. }

3

Translation:

"I wouldn't be caught **dead** in that outfit and neither should you."

"Put that down—you don't know where it's been!"

{

Referring mainly to objects found on the ground in public places—things like coins, candy, half-eaten sandwiches, and used chewing gum—this ism reflects every mom's pathological fear of germs.

}

4

"They're just jealous, that's all."

A time-honored but weak attempt to comfort a child who has been treated cruelly by his or her peers. This ism is often uttered through clenched teeth as Mom plans the untimely, slow, and painful death of her kid's tormenters.

"What did I just say?"

{ The child interprets this as a challenge over whether or not they are paying attention. But in most cases, the actual translation is, "I'm not testing your hearing. I have actually forgotten what I just said and I'm hoping you can tell me." }

"Don't forget your rubbers!"

In the fifties, this popular momism was a blunt, and often embarrassing, reminder for children to wear their galoshes (boots) in inclement weather. In those days, all moms believed that wet feet were the leading cause of colds, influenza, mumps, polio, mono, and most terminal diseases.

Today, the phrase has taken on a whole new meaning and is usually uttered by moms, under their breath, when their sons leave for college.

"Don't go out with a wet head, you'll catch pneumonia."

{ Like feet, wet heads are believed to be the second leading cause of the most dreaded diseases, especially the nefarious pneumonia. }

Note:

Next to head lice, pneumonia and its mysterious cousin, "walking pneumonia," continue to be a mother's worst nightmare in spite of modern antibiotics and other miracles of modern medicine.

"Pretty is as pretty does."

{ This is used with daughters as a postscript to such motherly advice as: }

"Pull your skirt **down**."

"Keep your legs **together**."

"*Comb* your **hair** out of your eyes."

"Stand up **straight**."

"Take your elbows **off** the table."

"Sit **up**, shoulders back."

"Pick up your **feet** when you **walk**."

"Horses sweat, men perspire, ladies glow."

{ An age-old ism intended to stop daughters (and sons) from using that unsavory word *sweat*. }

Unfortunately, this one has never really caught on, as you'll never hear anyone at the gym complain, "I'm glowing like a pig" or "You're working up a good glow!"

"Look it up in the dictionary!"

This ism is used to foster educational self-sufficiency, resourcefulness, and initiative.

Translation:

"Are you kidding? I have no idea how to spell **prestidigitation** and I'm too damned old to learn!"

"Imitation is the sincerest form of flattery."

This classic momism is usually spoken to pacify a child who is upset over being copied by a peer. It is only moderately effective and never works in reverse when one of Mom's peers shows up at a party wearing *her* dress, shoes, or haircut!

"You can't always tell a book by its cover."

Another way of saying "things aren't always as they seem," this is frequently used to prevent kids from becoming romantically involved with people who are too pretty or polite for their own good.

"I never talked to *my* mother like that!"

Translation:

14

"I **can't** think of a **snappy** comeback right now so I'm playing the *guilt* card . . . **again**."

"You're going to miss me when I'm gone!"

{ Yet another attempt to inflict guilt on a mis-behaving child, this subtly implies that if the offensive behavior doesn't cease and desist immediately, the mother's life expectancy could be dangerously reduced. }

"If Susie* jumped off a cliff, would you follow her?"

{ This all-time favorite is another maternal attempt to thwart peer pressure of any kind—and get Mom off the hook. It's usually used to rebuff typical kid arguments like: }

16

But **Susie** gets to stay out till twelve-thirty!

But Susie has her OWN phone line.

But *Susie's* mom lets her wear halter tops!

But **Susie** got her *nipples* pierced!

*Substitute any first name.

"Just wait till you have kids of your own."

Every mother knows the only way to gain complete parental restitution is for her kids to have kids of their own. Then, and only then, will they realize the sacrifice, pain, and suffering moms go through every day of their thankless lives.

"This place is a pigsty!"

{ This pathetic attempt at motivating children to improve their housekeeping skills usually falls on deaf ears, especially with urban urchins who think a pigsty is an eye infection in swine. }

"Where do you think you're living—in a barn?"

A mother's metaphorical response to a child who absentmindedly leaves the door open on a cold or hot day, it's too subliminal for most children to comprehend. The more effective retort is:

Close the damn door!

"Go out and play in traffic."

Translation:

"I have had **enough** of you for the **day**. **Don't** even *think* about coming back inside until I am *fully* medicated."

"Just be yourself."

Offered as a confidence booster before stressful occasions—first day of school, parties, big dates, job interviews—this ism tends to confuse the young person who isn't sure what "be yourself" truly means.

Translation for a son:

"Be *anyone* but your father."

For a daughter:

"Just be like **me**."

"Don't ever let me catch you doing that again."

{ Some would argue this classic momism sends a mixed message, which is: You can *do* it—I just don't want to *find out* about it. }

22

The underlying principle here is:
What Mom doesn't know won't hurt you.

"It's your money."

Frequently uttered with the same cautionary tone as "You'll be sorry," this one is used to prevent a child (young or old) from throwing away his or her hard-earned money on something frivolous, tasteless, or over-priced—like candy, flip-top hula girl dolls, or a Jaguar convertible.

"I'm going to give you until the count of three."

{ When Mom resorts to the dreaded three-count, chances are she's at the end of her rope and you'd be well advised to do what she says immediately. }

24

Note:

Of course, the savvy child knows he'll have more than three seconds to get the job done since most moms go into "stall mode" somewhere between "two-and-a-half" and "three":

"One . . . two . . . two and a half . . . two and three-quarters . . . don't make me say 'three' . . . two and seven-eighths . . . two and fifteen-sixteenths . . . don't make me say 'three' . . . I'm warning you . . . "

"Don't pick, it'll get infected."

Referring mainly to scabs, pimples, mosquito bites, and the like, this ominous warning has been used for generations to scare the bejesus out of kids. This ism is often accompanied by some outrageous story about a poor kid in Mississippi that picked a chigger bite on his foot and ended up having his entire leg amputated.

The operative word here is *infected*. Some moms manage to attach such a frightening connotation to the word that the first time a child actually does get an infection, he's likely to think he's a goner.

25

"Who are you going with? Do I know them?"

In a perfect world, all mothers would be able to obtain a full FBI background check on every one of their children's friends and acquaintances. Since this is impossible or, at the very least, impractical, many moms will drill their children for any revealing detail:

26

What do his **parents** do?

How did you **meet** her?

Where does he **live**?

Does she have a **police** record?

Any **tattoos** or *piercings*?

Can you get me a DNA **sample** before you go?

"Look at me when I'm talking to you."

Moms do not like to be ignored, especially when delivering a long, impassioned diatribe on a child's bad behavior. Maintaining eye contact is the only way a mom can tell if her message is getting through, even if the eyes in question seems to be glazing over into a zombielike state.

"Wipe that smile off your face before I do it for you."

{ Heaven help the child that dares to laugh while they're being scolded! }

28

There is nothing more maddening to an already angry mom than a child getting the giggles during a tongue lashing. This is to be avoided at all costs, lest the child receive the above threat.

"I brought you into this world, I can take you out."

{ Mothers make a lot of idle threats when they feel they're losing control. This is one of the more idle ones. }

Hopefully.

"Don't cross your eyes like that! They might stick!"

{ While there has never been any scientific proof that crossing your eyes can result in permanent strabismus, the very possibility usually prevents kids from doing it again. }

"You're going to put your eye out with that thing!"

(Again with the eyes!)

Often reserved for warnings about sharp objects like knitting needles, pencils, pick-up sticks, skewers, plastic swords, and the occasional rubber band, this momism conjures up disgusting and frightening images in the child's mind of eyeballs dangling from their sockets by thin threads.

"Don't sit too close to the television, it'll ruin your eyes."

(Yet *again* with the eyes!)

{ Another less-than-scientific cautionary note from Dr. Mom, this one seems to suggest that blindness is caused by Saturday-morning cartoon watching, MTV, and video games. }

"Eat your carrots, they're good for your eyesight."

Experts aren't sure why mothers are universally obsessed with their children's eyesight. Chances are, the high cost of glasses and contact lenses has a lot to do with it.

"Do you think your clothes are going to pick themselves up?"

This rhetorical question probably got the point across until the movie *Mary Poppins* came out. Now, after viewing the classic clean-up-the-nursery scene, kids can't help but think maybe clothes *do* pick themselves up and dance themselves into the closet to boot! All it takes is a spoonful of sugar!

Damn that Walt Disney.

"Just wait until your father gets home!"

Back in the days of stay-at-home moms and one-income families, this old chestnut was intended to strike fear in the hearts of misbehaving children. Anxiously waiting for Dad to walk in the door at 5:30 was usually more torturous than the subsequent punishment.

Today, with more mothers bringing home the bacon, you'll probably hear many a dad crying in frustration: "Just wait until your mother gets home!"

"There is nothing for nice girls to do past midnight."

Used as rationalization for imposing a twelve o'clock curfew on a teenaged daughter, this ism seems to suggest that "nice girls" turn evil at the stroke of midnight. Teenaged girls usually respond by saying a girl can be "bad" at any time of the day or night and, if they want to have sex, they can do it in the middle of the afternoon.

36

This line of reasoning does nothing to help their case with Mom and can, in fact, backfire in a major way.

"You made your bed, now lie in it."

{ This is another way of saying "You brought this on yourself" and is often followed by the dreaded "I told you so." }

Kids hate hearing this one.

That's why moms keep using it.

"'I don't know' is not an answer."

{ On any given day in any household in the universe where moms and kids cohabitate, you can hear a mother giving a kid the third degree: }

Mom: *Where* are you going tonight?
Kid: **I dunno.**
Mom: Well, **what** are you going to do?
Kid: **I dunno.**
Mom: Okay, **who** are you going with?
Kid: **I dunno.**
Mom: *"I don't know"* is **not** an answer!
Kid: **Whatever.**

There are few things more frustrating to a mother than the phrase "I dunno." But a dispassionate "whatever" can push her right over the edge.

"This hurts me more than it hurts you."

{ This age-old momism is used as a precursor to some form of punishment—a spanking, grounding, time-out, or earlier curfew. Moms do not like to deprive their children of anything and most punishments are, in fact, more painful to the mom than they are to the child. }

Unfortunately, most children
don't believe this until
they have kids of their own.

"What do you mean you can't find it? Where did you see it last?"

In their saner moments, most mothers realize the utter illogicality of these questions. Naturally, if the child could remember where she last saw the object in question, she would be able to locate it without hesitation.

That's why this particular ism is usually posed in the midst of sheer panic situations, such as:

The school bus is honking outside and the "Live Snakes of the Suburbs" science project is nowhere to be found.

40

Grandma dropped by for an unexpected visit and the Precious Moments statuette she gave at Christmas has mysteriously disappeared.

T minus ten minutes and counting until the orthodontist appointment and no sign of the retainer.

"Life isn't fair."

{ This is the standard retort to the child's complaint, "No fair!"

Most moms will leave it at that simple, three-word reply, but once in a while, the provoked mom will unleash a litany of woe at the unsuspecting child, such as: }

42

"Fair? Do you think varicose veins are fair? Or how about that rusty heap I drive you to school in every day? Is it fair I should still have to drive that thing while your dad gets a new SUV? Is it fair that the Thompsons down the street are in Jamaica right now while we're at home freezing our butts off in this weather? Is it fair that Max Factor discontinued the only shade of lipstick that ever looked good on me? Is that fair? And what about panty hose? What, pray tell, is fair about panty hose? Huh?"

When this happens, kids would be wise to quietly sneak out of the room. A rant like this could go on for days.

"Clean your plate. There are children starving in India."*

{ An admirable attempt to make children appreciate that they are lucky enough to be eating a hot meal, this guilt inducement often makes the child wonder why they couldn't just wrap up their helping of Tofu Surprise and FedEx it to the starving children in question. }

44

*Used interchangeably with Africa, China, Nicaragua, or any Third World country or domestic inner city.

"No means no!"

{ The purpose of this momism is to distinguish between the words *no* and *maybe*. Most kids know that when Mom says "maybe," then the answer is probably yes. But when Mom says "no," nine times out of ten she, in fact, *means* "no"... }

Unless, of course, she changes
her mind later to "maybe."

"Would you do that if the queen were here?"

{ An odd and questionably effective attempt to combat bad manners like talking with one's mouth full, putting one's elbows on the table, swearing, using one's shirt as a napkin, or countless other domestic offenses. }

46

Most kids realize that the chances of the queen, any queen, visiting their humble abode are extremely remote. (Unless you count Uncle Harry, who enjoys wearing Grandma's negligees once in a while.)

"Don't wear torn underwear. You never know when you might be in a car accident!"

This one ludicrously suggests that the worst thing that could possibly happen in an accident scenario is the emergency-room nurse discovering a rip or two in the victim's underwear and spreading the word to everyone in the ER:

"Doctor, we've got a thirteen-year-old male with a broken clavicle, blood pressure 100 over 60, possible internal bleeding. And check out those shabby shorts! What was his mother thinking?!"

"Don't forget to flush (or brush, floss, wipe, etc.)."

One of the many daunting responsibilities in a mother's life is to train her son(s) in the fine art of personal hygiene. This is easier said than done since most boys, until the approximate age of thirty, require constant daily reminders to perform the most basic of hygienic tasks. These momisms are used several times a day around most households.

Sometimes moms find it difficult to leave these warnings at home and may absentmindedly yell: "Don't forget to wipe!" as their young sons head for the rest room of a five-star restaurant.

48

"Shut the door— and *don't* slam it!"

{
There are few things more annoying to a mom than an open door. Open doors let flies, mice, and pesky neighbor kids in. They also let precious air-conditioned air out. This is why doors need to be closed at all times.
}

That said, a child's goal should be to achieve total silence when closing doors, as door slamming is another privilege reserved only for the mother.

"Be good—and don't do *anything* to embarrass your parents."

{
Used as a send-off to camp, parties, church outings, and such, this is a cautionary reminder that the behavior of a child always reflects on the parents, particularly the mother.
}

50

"No child of *mine* would do something like that."

{ Another way of saying, "This is unacceptable behavior in our family," this declaration can be confusing to the child who is already questioning why he doesn't look a thing like his parents or siblings. }

"There must've been some kind of mix-up in the hospital . . . this can't be *my* child!"

{ Moms use this when a child has done something out of character—for better or for worse—like cleaning his room without being asked or blowing his little sister's favorite Barbie doll to smithereens with a cherry bomb. }

52

It is never a good idea to raise the possibility of a hospital mix-up, even in jest. The impressionable child might take this idea and run with it, especially if he bears a resemblance to a celebrity or the guy down the block.

"Five minutes of pleasure is not worth a lifetime of hell."

This priceless nugget is often employed to dissuade curious teenagers from participating in any risky activity—sex, speeding, alcohol, drugs, or in some cases, fried foods

"No, you can't go steady! You *know* what that leads to."

"Going steady," while absent from today's vernacular, was considered by older moms as the first step toward sexual intimacy, a point of no return.

Nowadays, wistful moms long for the days when all they had to worry about was their daughters going steady. At least that meant they only had one partner!

"How can you sleep in an unmade bed?"

To a child, this is one of the most ludicrous questions ever posed by an adult. Because, as kid logic would have it, one must *unmake* a bed to get in the bed to sleep—therefore, why make the bed in the first place?

"Don't make me tell you again."

Every mom has her own "reminder threshold"—the number of times it takes to give an order before it is carried out. Some moms will simply ask once and expect it to be done. (These are the rare breeds.) Others will be content to ask twice, thrice, even five times before she runs out of patience. When a mother says, "Don't make me tell you again" it should be taken as a serious threat.

56

"Am I talking to a brick wall?"

Another attempt to satisfy a mom's desperate need to be heard by her offspring, this
momism is usually used when attempting to
carry on a conversation with young children
while the TV is on the Cartoon Network.

57

"Money does *not* grow on trees."

{ More of a lament than sage advice, this ism is typically followed by a mom's silent inner monologue: }

58

"Boy, do I *wish* money grew on trees because, if it did, I certainly wouldn't be wearing these ratty old sweatpants and three-month-old dark roots. And, for once, you kids might volunteer to rake the yard!"

"You take after your father!" ("You get that from your father's side of the family.")

Rarely intended as a compliment, this accusatory remark uses genetics, and particularly the Y chromosome, to explain a child's undesirable behavior or personality traits, especially burping, passing gas, talking with a full mouth, cussing, spitting, unabashedly scratching one's private parts, and hogging the remote control.

"When you're the mother then you can be the boss."

Normally used in response to an adolescent girl's snappy comeback: "You're not the boss of me!," this ism gently reminds the little bundle of hormones that only after one endures nine months of pregnancy and several hours of painful labor (*after* one is married, mind you) will one truly deserve the title of *boss*.

60

"I'm not here to entertain you."

Translation:

"You have a **five**-thousand-dollar play structure in the backyard, a **big-screen** TV, dozens of *video* games, 2,975,221 Lego pieces on the floor of your closet, two scooters, a bike, and **six** kids your age living within two hundred **feet** of our *front* door. How can you possibly barge in here, interrupt my **Oprah** time, and complain: 'There's nothing to do!'?"

61

"There's no shame in being poor, but there is shame in being dirty!"

{ It's a universal fact: Moms hate dirt. And there's nothing more terrifying than a child leaving home in a less than clean condition. That's why moms tend to overreact at the sight of stained shirts, grass-stained pants, or dirty fingernails. }

Girls understand this.

Boys never will.

"You'll never live to see sixteen!"

If mothers had their way, children wouldn't leave the house each morning without a full set of pads, crash helmet, safety goggles, mouth guard, and a germ-impervious bubble enveloping their bodies. Alas, such an outfit would never make it past the junior high fashion police. So kids are forced to face the world with only their common sense to protect them.

63

That's why most kids are just accidents waiting to happen.

"It smells like something's died in here!"

It is a well-known fact that moms possess a keener sense of smell than all other humans on the planet. A mother's nose can detect alcohol on the breath, cigarette smoke on clothing, and, most impressive, spoiled food or other substances rotting in a teenager's room. (A few exceptionally gifted moms can actually pinpoint the expiration dates of certain molding foods. Example: "Substance: yogurt; brand: Dannon; flavor: banana-strawberry; expiration date, 4/30/2001.")

Chances are slim that something will actually die in a teenager's room, but the smell of curdled milk and molding ham sandwiches can often be mistaken for decomposing flesh.

"I worry about you."

The mother of all understatements, this is a mom's futile attempt to make a child understand that worrying is a mom's 24/7 scourge. It's also the reason for every wrinkle on her face, dimple in her thigh, and gray hair on her head. (In fact, it is maternal worry that keeps the cosmetic, weight-loss, and hair-color industries in business.)

"I hate having you drive alone at night."

When her child is out driving alone at night, a mother's already fertile imagination jumps into overdrive. Every siren heard in the distance conjures up horrifying images of bloody car wrecks, broken glass, twisted metal, torn limbs, and roadside CPR. And with every passing hour, the horrors increase until some moms reach a full-blown psychotic episode that causes them to phone the police, highway patrol, and ambulance service. These episodes usually peak just as the child is pulling into the driveway.

"I don't care if you *want* to . . . do it anyway!"

The average mom uses approximately 60 percent of her vocabulary issuing commands: "Do your homework. Eat your vegetables. Wash your face. Brush your teeth. Make your bed. Clean your room. Take a bath. Turn off the TV." And so on.

The average child responds to these commands 72 percent of the time, by saying, "I don't want to!"

In 88 percent of the cases, the average mom will counter this response with the above momism. If she is premenstrual, she'll add a cuss word nine times out of ten.

"There's enough dirt in those ears to grow potatoes!"

The decline of Q-tips sales proves that clean ears have taken a downward turn on the list of maternal priorities. Still, there are those ever-vigilant moms who still inspect a child's ears before they go out in public. Pity these children, as they will never put anything over on their mothers in their lifetimes.

"What would you do if I wasn't here?"

Intended to make a child stop and think about how much Mom does for him each day, this rhetorical question sometimes invokes a kid's ultimate fantasy . . .

69

"**What** *would* **I do if she wasn't here? Let's see . . . Invite everyone over, including that hot babe from chemistry, crank up the stereo, call Pizza Hut delivery, MTV 24/7 . . . How long did you say you'd be gone, Mom?"**

"After you pick up your room, make your bed, brush your teeth, and comb your hair, *then* you can go out to play."

70

{ There was a time when "going out to play" was the carrot at the end of the stick, the only sure fire motivator to get a child to finish his or her chores. }

Nowadays, being forced to "pick up your room" can become a real adventure as the child may uncover video games, DVDs, and toys he didn't know he had!

"Don't say *shut up!*"

{ No mother worth her salt would permit her child to say "shut up." }

Mom reserves that privilege for herself, to use on Dad.

"Close your mouth when you're eating—you look like a cow chewing her cud!"

{ This esteem-affirming statement is usually meant as a reminder to a child to keep one's mouth closed when one chews. }

72

Most people, including the author, are not sure what cud really is! But it sounds gross, so it works.

"Be good—but if you can't be good, be careful."

{ The ultimate parental loophole, this ism acknowledges that kids will occasionally succumb to temptation and do something they shouldn't do. This momism can be translated for several applications: }

73

Don't have **sex!** (But if you do, don't get **pregnant!**)

Don't *drink!* (But if you do, don't **drive!**)

Don't do **drugs!** (But if you **do**, don't get arrested!)

Don't **speed!** (But if you do, don't get a **ticket!**)

"Eat the crust. It will make your hair curly and your teeth white."

74

One of the most hotly debated issues in the field of home economics today is the nutritional value of crust. In one camp are the moms who insist that crust is good for you for the cosmetic reasons mentioned above. The other camp consists of the mothers who painstakingly cut the crust off their kids' peanut butter and jelly sandwiches. (These are probably the same people who refused to eat the crust when they were kids.) There's no definitive answer as to which group is right. Just don't ever get them together in the same playgroup!

"I'm on strike!"

Three little words that strike fear into the hearts of fathers and kids alike, this is a mom's declaration that she has had it "up to here" with laundry, cooking, cleaning, carpooling, and the rest of the mundane chores that occupy her time.

Fortunately for the rest of the family, such "strikes" only last a couple of minutes, after which Mom's guilt inevitably kicks in. But there have been instances of prolonged work stoppages by mothers who have literally walked out of their homes and manned picket lines in their own backyards. When this happens, families would be well advised to negotiate a settlement before Mom makes it onto the six o'clock news.

"Remember where you come from."

Commonly used to remind the child that he or she comes from good stock and is expected to behave accordingly, this momism can also be useful for the directionally challenged child who tends to get lost just walking home from school.

"Do as I say, not as I do."

{ This interesting disclaimer is an adult's neat, one-size-fits-all counter to the following observations by kids: }

But *you're* not wearing *your* seatbelt!

But *you* **smoke**!

But *you* drink **beer**!

But *you're* not eating *your* vegetables!

But *you* and *Dad* stay up late and make noise in *your* bedroom!

"What will the neighbors think?"

Though they'll never admit it, moms worry about appearances—especially in their neighborhoods and PTAs. That's why mothers are so obsessed with things like bikes left out in the yard, junk cars in the driveway, and husbands going out to fetch the newspaper in boxer shorts, black socks, and sandals.

"First marry for love, then marry for money."

Mothers are nothing if not practical crea-
tures. Even the most romantic and idealistic
of them will admit that her comfort zone is
greatly increased if a future son- or daughter-
in-law has a healthy trust fund and is heir to
the family fortune.

"I love you all equally."

{
This is Mom's pat answer to the dreaded
question: "Who do you love the most?"
   Some inexperienced moms will add the
caveat: " ... but for different reasons."
}

A word of warning:
Don't even go there.

"Sure, your brother has book smarts, but *you* have street smarts."

{ Unfortunately, there can only be one "smartest kid" in the family, and this momism is intended to assuage the ego of the less brain-endowed. }

Moms should be careful to explain that "street smarts" means "common sense" . . . not the natural ability to sell crack from the front seat of your car.

"When I was a little girl . . ."

A prelude to one of mom's precious girlhood stories about the time she got Chatty Cathy's hair stuck in the drain, the joys of her annual backyard carnivals, or how she always wanted to fill out a sweater like Annette Funicello.

82

When you hear this one, don't fight it. Just sit back and enjoy the tale . . . again!

"What do you need, an engraved invitation? Sit down and eat!"

When a mom resists the temptation to order out, then slaves over a hot stove to prepare a delicious meal that strictly adheres to the ever-changing food pyramid nutrition model, she expects her family to run to the table like stampeding cattle the moment she announces "Dinner's ready!" Anything less is, well, insulting.

A little advice: If you want to make Mom's day, the next time she yells "Dinner's ready!," make a mad dash to the table licking your lips and shouting "Me first!" And if you can leave a family member in your wake, so much the better.

"Act your age."

Here's a momism that can mean completely different things in different situations.

To a twelve-year-old squirming in church, it means: "Act like an adult!"

To the same twelve-year-old caught kissing a first crush, it means: "Act like a child!"

"You're not fat.
You just have big bones."

{ Some of the all-time greatest rationalizations are passed down through the generations by well-intentioned mothers. The "big bones" rationale is one of the best. It is typically used by the mom who firmly believes that she herself is not fat, just cursed by bones bigger than Tyrannosaurus Rex's. }

"You have a cute little figure."

{ This classic momism is used to pacify anxious, late-blooming girls who complain they're the last in their class to develop boobs and hips. }

Translation:

"So you **look** like a stick! **Enjoy** it **while** it lasts."

"What have I done to deserve this?"

A flagrant cry for help, this ism should be a huge red flag to everyone in the household that Mom is in desperate need of tea, sympathy, and a girls-only weekend at a very expensive spa.

"Stop hiding that beautiful face."

{ Moms of today can tolerate bleached, punked-out hairstyles, weird tattoos, and multiple piercings. But when a child's hair hangs in her face, a mom cannot be responsible for her actions. }

The urge to push the hair out of a child's eyes is an uncontrollable biological reflex, no different from gagging, sneezing, or hiccupping. No mother on earth can resist it.

"I hope someday you have children just like you."

{ This multipurpose momism can be used for positive or negative reinforcement. }

In her proudest moments, say after her child scores a 1280 on the **SAT**, a mom throws her arms around a child and says, "I hope someday you have children just (as wonderful) as you."

Used, say, after traipsing down to the police station at two in the morning to bail out a son after TPing the principal's house, "I hope someday you have children just (as incredibly *stupid*) as you."

"Two wrongs do not make a right."

{
This ancient adage is applied when a child has lied to cover up another misdeed—like stealing, staying out past curfew, or snarfing the last piece of Mom's apple pie.
}

90

"Don't talk
with your mouth full!"

{ Among the top five horrors in any mother's mind is the fear that her child will be sitting at someone else's dinner table and attempt to express his opinion with a mouth full of lasagna. }

"Am I embarrassing you?"

Moms have an uncanny knack for questioning the obvious.

92

Because after a certain age, no matter what a mother is doing or saying—or how cool she is dressed— her child will be mortified just by her very existence.

"Stand up straight or you'll get a hump in your back and no boy will ever ask you out."

This antiquated momism seems like nonsense to the young girls of today . most of whom know that dowager's hump is caused by calcium deficiency and genetics, not by bad posture.

Thus, moms would be well advised to use a more modern alternative with a different approach:

Stand up straight. You'll thrust your chest out, increasing the size of your bust by two inches. Then the boys will be standing in line to ask you out.

"You can pick your friends, but you can't pick your relatives."

{
Typically uttered on the way to reunions, weddings, and other family gatherings, this ominous ism is intended to fend off a child's complaints about spending yet another day with stinky Aunt Marge or Uncle Lenny the mime.
}

94

"This, too, shall pass."

{ An old standby, this is the ism to try when no other ism will do. }

Translation:

"Get **over** it."

"I'm not just talking to hear my own voice."

{ But every once in a while, especially in families of four or more, moms talk just to hear themselves think. }

"You must think rules are made to be broken."

It is imperative for moms to understand that, of course, kids think rules are made to be broken. And until they find a second career that's just as rewarding, this will be their life's work.

Knowing that is half the battle.

"Put a quarter in your shoe in case you need to call home."

An old favorite, this momism has given way to the modern alternative:

"Take your cell phone in case you need to call home . . . *but only in emergencies!* We only have so many free minutes!"

"As long as you live under my roof, you'll do as I say."

{ Home is a mother's only true domain. And no matter how old a child may get, Mom gets to make the rules for all who dwell there. }

This is why kids tend to leave home
around the age of eighteen.

"Is that a threat or a promise? ... Don't let the door hit you in the rear ... I'll help you pack ... Write when you get work!"

100

Little Johnny has just thrown the tantrum of the decade. He stomps to his room, slams the door, and screams, "I'm running away from home and I'm never coming back!" That's when Mom launches into "reverse psychology" mode, all the while hoping her plan doesn't backfire because she just doesn't have the strength for a run to the bus station at rush hour.

"No use crying over spilt milk."

{ This venerable momism is an expression that means: What's done is done. It is not meant to be taken literally. }

Unless, of course, an entire gallon of the milk in question has just been spilt over your newly carpeted family room floor. Then, a little crying is called for.

"You can't make a silk purse out of a sow's ear."

{ No one is entirely sure what this momism means, although it is frequently used to illustrate the futility of trying to change a no-good man into a good one. }

If you know the exact translation,
please contact the author.

"You catch more flies with honey than with vinegar."

Intended to promote sweetness over bitterness in a child's personality, the meaning of this metaphor is lost on most children who wonder why you'd want to catch flies in the first place.

"Because I said so, that's why!"

{ "But why?" may be the most irritating question on earth, especially when asked by an unrelentingly whining child in Kmart's checkout line. The mother-tot exchange often goes like this: }

104

Child: Mommy, can I buy some candy?

Mom: No.

Child: But why?

Mom: Because it's bad for your teeth.

Child (getting louder): But **whyyyyy**?

Mom: Because **sugar** causes tooth **decay**.

Child (**agitated** now): But whyyyyyyyy?

Mom: Because it turns to **plaque** which **eats** into the **enamel.**

Child (in full whine mode) But *whyyyyyyyyyy*?

Mom: Because **plaque,** when left unchecked, cre-
ates **bacteria,** which contains **acid** that
eats into the tooth's hard **surface . . .**

Child (breaking the sound **barrier** now): But
whyyyyyyyyyyyy?

It is strongly recommended at this point,
before other Kmart shoppers vault over the
conveyor belts and take matters into their
own hands, that the mother say, with all the
authority she can command: "Because I said
so, you little putz, that's why!"

"If you can't say something nice, don't say anything at all."

{ Good moms use the above ism to teach children that gossip is wrong.

Bad moms use the alternative: "If you can't say something nice, come sit next to me!" }

(There's a little "bad mom" in all of us, I'm afraid.)

"Don't make me come in there!"

Translation:

"I don't **know** what you're **doing** behind that door. *And* I don't **want** to know. But if I keep hearing those blood-curdling **screams,** I'm going to have to get up **off** this couch and miss God-knows-how-many minutes of **Oprah** and Dr. Phil. And then there will be **hell** to pay, *mister!*"

"I love you."

(No translation necessary.)

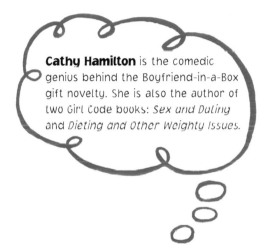

Cathy Hamilton is the comedic genius behind the Boyfriend-in-a-Box gift novelty. She is also the author of two Girl Code books: *Sex and Dating* and *Dieting and Other Weighty Issues*.